UEFA
EURO2020

FA ___ TLE

MAY 21   DATE DUE   796.33

0 9 FEB 2022

PRINTED IN U.S.A.

The Library
Stewart's Melville College

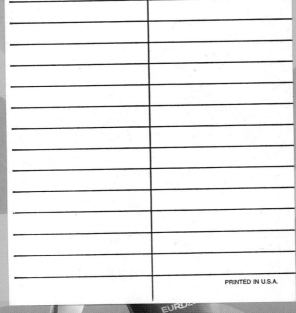

EURO20

TM

STEWART'S MELVILLE COLLEGE

D0336292

CONTENTS

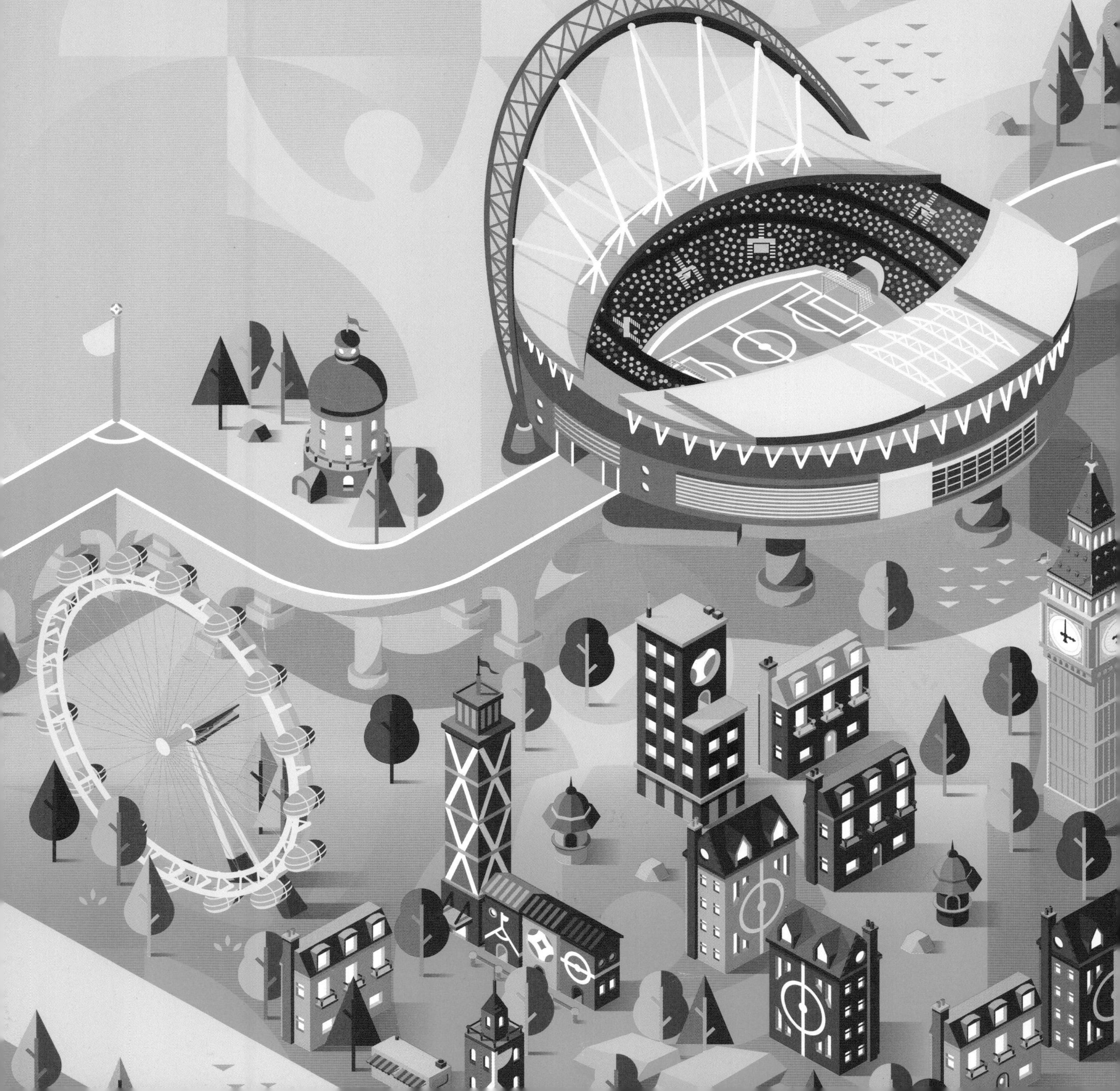

UEFA EURO 2020 KICK-OFF!

The biggest continental football competition Europe has ever seen kicks off on 11 June, a year after it was postponed in 2020 following the COVID-19 pandemic. For the first time, the exciting EURO finals take place across 12 different countries, including England, Germany, Italy, Scotland and Spain. Millions of fans around the world will be treated to a festival of football packed with superstars, goals and awesome action.

Although a year later than planned, EURO 2020 is special as it celebrates the 60th anniversary of this famous event. The first EURO was held in 1960, in which the USSR (Soviet Union, now represented by Russia) beat Yugoslavia in the final. Sixty-one years on, the competition will see 24 teams battle it out for a place in the final, due to take place at Wembley Stadium in London on 11 July 2021.

PORTU-GOAL!

Captained by the superstar Cristiano Ronaldo, Portugal claimed the UEFA EURO 2016 crown and their first major trophy thanks to an extra-time goal from forward Éder. The win was extra sweet as they beat the hosts and favourites, France, at the famous Stade de France in Paris.

LEFT: Portugal celebrate their triumph at UEFA EURO 2016 after beating France in the final.

SUPER SILVERWARE

The big prize on offer is the Henri Delaunay trophy. Standing 60cm tall, weighing 8kg and made from sterling silver, the cup is named in honour of the first general secretary of UEFA. Portugal, Spain, Greece and France have all lifted the cup in the 21st century. Which team will get their hands on the gleaming trophy in 2021?

60cm

LEFT: Star players featuring at EURO 2020 (*L to R*): Sergio Ramos (ESP), Manuel Neuer (GER) and Antoine Griezmann (FRA).

WORK IT OUT

The first UEFA EURO 2020 match is set to be played at the Olimpico in Rome on 11 June 2021. There are 51 matches to be played in total during the tournament, beginning with the group stage games followed by the round of 16, quarter-finals, semi-finals and final. See pages 62–63 for a closer look at the games and venues.

The 24 nations competing in UEFA EURO 2020 had to battle through a qualifying stage that started in March 2019. During qualifying, 55 sides, put into one of ten groups of either five or six teams, played home and away matches against others in their group. The top two teams qualified from each group, taking the first 20 spots. A series of play-offs in October and November 2020 decided who took the other four places. Teams reached the play-off stage because of their final positions in their UEFA Nations League group in 2018. The four play-off winners were Hungary, North Macedonia, Scotland and Slovakia.

RIGHT: Belgium midfielder Kevin De Bruyne launches a thunderous strike against Scotland in UEFA EURO 2020 qualifying.

ABOVE: France's Kylian Mbappé *(R)* battles for the ball against Iceland's Hördur Magnússon during a UEFA EURO 2020 qualifying match.

THE GROUP STAGE

Group matches run between 11 and 23 June. The 24 teams are placed in six groups of four, with each country playing three games in their group. The top two teams from each group, plus the four best third-placed teams, go through to the round of 16. Fans love the fun and frantic feeling of group games at a UEFA European Championship – on some days there are four games kicking off! The last games in each group kick off at the same time.

THE KNOCKOUT STAGES

This is when the tension and excitement goes up a level – from here on teams must win all their games! The round of 16 takes place from 26 to 29 June, with a different city hosting each of the eight matches. These games could go to extra time and penalties. The four quarter-finals and two semi-finals will then determine which two nations go head-to-head in the final for the Henri Delaunay Cup on 11 July.

MEET THE HOSTS

UEFA has chosen 12 fabulous football nations to host the sporting party this summer! This unique idea will allow many more fans from different nations to be closer to the action. Each host nation will stage at least four games, including group stage and knockout matches. The host countries are Azerbaijan, Denmark, England, Germany, Hungary, Italy, Netherlands, Republic of Ireland, Romania, Russia, Scotland and Spain.

RIGHT: A young England fan cheers on his team by waving a flag bearing the famous "Three Lions" crest.

GREAT GUESTS

Five of these 12 nations have staged the EURO finals in the past. Belgium and the Netherlands co-hosted the event in 2000. The *Oranje*, as the Dutch team are fondly nicknamed, were crowned champions at the 1988 finals. Three-time winners Spain were hosts in 1964 and since then Italy, Germany and England have all staged the epic event.

DEBUT DELIGHT

Russia was the home for the 2018 FIFA World Cup, but this is the first time the huge country has been chosen as one of the hosts for a EURO finals. Elsewhere, the passion of fans in Scotland and the Republic of Ireland will be matched by supporters in Azerbaijan, Denmark, Hungary and Romania as they all stage finals for the very first time. Turn over to find out more about the stadiums and cities selected.

BELOW: Fans of Germany show their support and enjoy the atmosphere before their team takes to the field for kick-off.

ABOVE: Russia celebrate with their fans after beating Cyprus 1-0 in the EURO 2020 qualifiers in 2019.

BIG CELEBRATION

Right across the continent, from cities as widespread as Dublin and Baku, football fans are ready for the UEFA EURO 2020 party to begin. Because of the delayed start from June 2020, the excitement is now even greater and supporters are eager to see Europe's superstars go head to head. This unique event will live long in the memory of the millions watching around the world.

SUPER STADIUMS

It is time to take a look at the 12 super stadiums that are staging the UEFA EURO 2020 matches. The tournament is spread across iconic grounds like Wembley Stadium and Hampden Park, as well as new and modern venues such as the Puskás Aréna and the Saint Petersburg Stadium. Get ready for a guided tour of these great footballing venues!

OLIMPICO IN ROME
Country: Italy
City: Rome **Capacity:** 68,000
UEFA EURO 2020 matches:
3 x Group A, 1 x quarter-final

Home to rival Serie A clubs Lazio and Roma, the Olimpico in Rome is where UEFA EURO 2020 begins. The atmosphere inside the arena will be buzzing when Group A's opening fixture kicks off on 11 June. The Olimpico in Rome is world famous for holding big games since 1953. It staged the 1968 finals and the UEFA Champions League final four times in total.

BAKU OLYMPIC STADIUM
Country: Azerbaijan
City: Baku **Capacity:** 69,000
UEFA EURO 2020 matches:
3 x Group A, 1 x quarter-final

Azerbaijan has a long footballing history. In fact, the ceremony to start building the Baku Olympic Stadium (*below*) in June 2011 also doubled up as a celebration of the 100th anniversary of football in Azerbaijan! In 2019, this grand venue staged the UEFA Europa League final clash between London clubs Chelsea and Arsenal.

SAINT PETERSBURG STADIUM
Country: Russia
City: Saint Petersburg
Capacity: 61,000
UEFA EURO 2020 matches:
3 x Group B, 1 x quarter-final

If you watched the 2018 FIFA World Cup then you will recognise Saint Petersburg Stadium. Built on the eve of the tournament, its eye-catching design has been likened to that of a spaceship! Packed with modern features, such as a sliding pitch and retractable roof, fans can enjoy the Group B clashes and quarter-final on 2 July in style.

PARKEN STADIUM
Country: Denmark
City: Copenhagen
Capacity: 38,000
UEFA EURO 2020 matches:
3 x Group B, 1 x round of 16

Denmark's biggest football arena is actually the smallest of all the venues at UEFA EURO 2020, with a potential to have around 38,000 fans inside the ground. But what it lacks in size it will certainly make up for in atmosphere! The stadium was completed in 1992 and staged European club football finals in 1994 and 2000.

JOHAN CRUIJFF ARENA
Country: Netherlands
City: Amsterdam **Capacity:** 54,000
UEFA EURO 2020 matches:
3 x Group C, 1 x round of 16

Opened in 1996 and home to the illustrious Dutch club, Ajax, the stadium was the the first in Europe to feature a sliding roof over the pitch. The ground was renamed the Johan Cruijff ArenA in 2018 in honour of the brilliant Netherlands and Ajax forward, who passed away two years earlier. In 2000, the stadium staged five EURO finals matches.

NATIONAL ARENA BUCHAREST
Country: Romania
City: Bucharest; **Capacity:** 54,000
UEFA EURO 2020 matches:
3 x Group C, 1 x round of 16

Opened in 2011, the National Arena Bucharest (below) famously staged the UEFA Europa League final clash between Atlético Madrid and Athletic Club just a year later. This stadium also boasts a sliding roof, which could be potentially raised by the 54,000 supporters hoping to cheer on their teams when the four UEFA EURO 2020 fixtures kick off this summer!

WEMBLEY STADIUM
Country: England
City: London **Capacity:** 90,000
UEFA EURO 2020 matches:
3 x Group D, 1 x round of 16,
2 x semi-finals, final

As the setting for seven UEFA EURO 2020 games in total, including both semi-finals and the final, Wembley Stadium (above) is the headline venue this summer. The legendary stadium staged the EURO '96 final, but that was before the ground was rebuilt into a hi-tech and modern footballing venue. Lit up at night, the huge arch spanning the pitch is an impressive sight.

HAMPDEN PARK
Country: Scotland
City: Glasgow **Capacity:** 51,000
UEFA EURO 2020 matches:
3 x Group D, 1 x round of 16

Not many stadiums in Europe can boast the glorious history of Hampden Park, located in Scotland's largest city. Famously, in 1937, it drew a crowd of almost 150,000 for a match between Scotland and England! In 1999, Hampden Park was modernised into an all-seater ground, and three years later it held the 2002 UEFA Champions League final between Real Madrid and Bayer Leverkusen.

DUBLIN ARENA
Country: Republic of Ireland
City: Dublin **Capacity:** 51,000
UEFA EURO 2020 matches:
3 x Group E, 1 x round of 16

Hosting EURO matches for the first time, the city will come alive during the four fixtures scheduled to take place at the Dublin Arena in June. Home to the Republic of Ireland national team since 2011, the stadium holds over 50,000 spectators and creates an amazing atmosphere for big games.

SAN MAMÉS STADIUM
Country: Spain
City: Bilbao **Capacity:** 53,000
UEFA EURO 2020 matches:
3 x Group E, 1 x round of 16

Built in 2013, the stadium in Bilbao perhaps rivals the Football Arena Munich as the tournament's most colourful stadium because its exterior can also be illuminated, which offers a spectacular sight at night! The venue might not match the size of grounds in Barcelona or Madrid but its splendour and history make it the ideal place to stage the four UEFA EURO 2020 fixtures in Spain.

FOOTBALL ARENA MUNICH
Country: Germany
City: Munich **Capacity:** 70,000
UEFA EURO 2020 matches:
3 x Group F, 1 x quarter-final

Germany has a long history of hosting the biggest international football events, which include the 1988 EUROs and two FIFA World Cups. Built in 2005, the Football Arena Munich is a visually striking and futuristic-looking ground, with an exterior that can be lit by 16 million LEDs. The four fixtures the venue will host all promise to be occasions to remember.

PUSKÁS ARÉNA
Country: Hungary
City: Budapest **Capacity:** 65,000
UEFA EURO 2020 matches:
3 x Group F, 1 x round of 16

There was only one footballer that Hungary could name its ace new stadium after – Ferenc Puskás – national and Real Madrid superstar of the 1950s and '60s. Opened in 2019, the venue (below) stands on the site of the old Nepstadion (People's Stadium) in Budapest. During UEFA EURO 2020 it will stage three Group F games and a round of 16 match.

CELEBRATING 60 YEARS

UEFA is hosting the 2020 European Football Championship in several nations as a "romantic" one-off event to celebrate the 60th birthday (reached in 2020) of the tournament. Let's take a look back at some of the major highlights from past EURO finals.

GOAL KING

Cristiano Ronaldo has scored a joint-record nine goals at EURO finals stretching across tournaments in 2016, 2012, 2008 and 2004. He shares the record with France's Michel Platini.

LEFT: Portugal's Cristiano Ronaldo celebrates his goal against Hungary at EURO 2016.

RIGHT: France star Michel Platini on the ball v Portugal at the 1984 EURO finals.

YOUNGEST AND OLDEST

The past two EURO finals saw the youngest and oldest players make appearances in the tournament. In 2016, Hungary keeper Gábor Király played at the age of 40 years and 74 days. Jetro Willems was just 18 years and 71 days old when he featured for the Netherlands at UEFA EURO 2012.

FINAL FACT

Spain hold the record for achieving the largest margin of victory in the UEFA European Championship final. In 2012, the team defeated Italy 4-0.

GREAT GERMANY

Germany and West Germany can proudly lay claim to a number of EURO records. Across the record 12 EURO final tournaments they've contested, the three-time winners have netted a record 72 goals, played 49 matches and collected 26 wins!

FAST BLAST

The record for the quickest goal from kick-off is held by Russia's Dmitri Kirichenko. At EURO 2004, Kirichenko scored after just 67 seconds against Greece. Russia went on to win 2-1.

LEFT: Spain's David Villa celebrates his goal against Russia at EURO 2008.

HAT-TRICK HEROES

Only seven players have netted a hat-trick (three goals in a single game) in a EURO match. The last to achieve this was Spain striker David Villa, whose goals helped *La Roja* beat Russia 4-1 in a group stage match at UEFA EURO 2008.

TOURNAMENT TIME

In total, 17 players have made appearances at four EURO finals. These include Gianluigi Buffon (Italy), Zlatan Ibrahimović (Sweden), Peter Schmeichel (Denmark) and Petr Čech (Czech Republic). Spain's Iker Casillas played in EURO finals in 2012, 2008 and 2004, and though he was in the squad in 2000 and 2016, he did not play.

HIGH FIVE

Only two nations have recorded five wins at a single EURO final tournament. France have managed it three times – in 1984, 2000 and 2016. In 2008, Spain secured a victory in five of their six matches.

SPEEDY SPOT KICK

The Republic of Ireland's Robbie Brady struck a quick-fire penalty against France at EURO 2016. He scored from the spot just 118 seconds after the round of 16 game began! Sadly his team lost 2-1.

ABOVE: Robbie Brady takes a spot kick to give the Republic of Ireland an early lead against France at EURO 2016.

FINAL GLORY

In the history of EURO tournaments, ten nations have enjoyed the special feeling of lifting the Henri Delaunay trophy to become champions. Germany and Spain have a hat-trick of titles and France have enjoyed double delight in the final.

RIGHT: Denmark's Brian Laudrup skips past a challenge during the final against Germany at EURO '92

 UEFA EURO 2016
Champions: Portugal
Runners-up: France
Portugal took the title for the first time with their extra-time win over France. It was perhaps a surprise victory as they had begun slowly with three draws in the group stage matches.

UEFA EURO 2012
Champions: Spain
Runners-up: Italy
These two football giants met in the opening Group C match, which ended 1-1. They both progressed to the final, where Spain hit top gear to register an emphatic 4-0 win!

UEFA EURO 2008
Champions: Spain
Runners-up: Germany
A single first-half strike from forward Fernando Torres was enough to see the stylish Spain team hold off Germany in the final in Vienna, Austria.

 UEFA EURO 2004
Champions: Greece
Runners-up: Portugal
A header from Angelos Charisteas saw Greece emerge victorious over the favourites, and hosts, Portugal 1-0 in Lisbon. Greece also beat Portugal in the opening game of the tournament!

UEFA EURO 2000
Champions: France
Runners-up: Italy
Perhaps the most breathtaking EURO final ever! France equalised in stoppage time and then grabbed a sudden death golden goal thanks to David Trezeguet, sending France fans into a frenzy of jubilation.

 UEFA EURO '96
Champions: Germany
Runners-up: Czech Republic
The first golden goal in the history of the EURO finals was scored by Germany. Substitute striker Oliver Bierhoff levelled the score in normal time before his historic winner in extra time.

UEFA EURO '92
Champions: Denmark
Runners-up: Germany
Denmark were late entrants into the tournament but surprised the world by ending up as European champions! Their 2-0 win in the final came thanks to strikes by John Jensen and Kim Vilfort.

1988 EURO FINALS

Champions: Netherlands
Runners-up: USSR

The Netherlands' only international trophy came in style, with legends like Ruud Gullit, Marco van Basten and Ronald Koeman strutting their stuff. Van Basten's famous volley helped the Dutch to a 2-0 win in the final.

1984 EURO FINALS

Champions: France
Runners-up: Spain

Held in France, fans of *Les Bleus* will always remember this action-packed EURO finals. Their 2-0 win against Spain gave them their first big trophy on the international stage.

1980 EURO FINALS

Champions: West Germany
Runners-up: Belgium

West Germany left it late to seal the title in 1980, with an 88th-minute goal from Horst Hrubesch that gave them a 2-1 win over a battling Belgium side.

1976 EURO FINALS

Champions: Czechoslovakia
Runners-up: West Germany

A late goal from West Germany forced the tense final into extra time. The game eventually went to penalties, with Czechoslovakia keeping their cool to come through 5-3 from the shoot-out.

1972 EURO FINALS

Champions: West Germany
Runners-up: USSR

Making their second appearance at a UEFA European Championship, West Germany played a powerful style of football that saw them lift the cup! They beat the USSR 3-0.

1968 EURO FINALS

Champions: Italy
Runners-up: Yugoslavia

The first and only time a EURO final went to a replay happened in 1968. After a 1-1 draw in the first game, Italy took the prize for the first time with a 2-0 victory in Rome.

1964 EURO FINALS

Champions: Spain
Runners-up: USSR

Only four competed at the 1964 EURO finals: Denmark, Hungary, Spain and USSR. Spain emerged the strongest, recording a 2-1 semi-final win and then a 2-1 victory in the final to take the title and EURO glory.

1960 EURO FINALS

Champions: USSR
Runners-up: Yugoslavia

The USSR (Soviet Union, now represented by Russia) won the honour of being crowned the first European champions when the tournament made its debut in 1960. They came from behind to win 2-1 after extra time at the Parc des Princes in Paris.

RIGHT: The Netherlands' Ruud Gullit *(L)* and France's Didier Deschamps *(R)* are two famous winners of the Henri Delaunay trophy.

LEGENDARY EURO WINNERS

Sergio Ramos
Winner: 2012, 2008

Rainer Bonhof
Winner: 1980, 1972

Ruud Gullit
Winner: 1988

Cristiano Ronaldo
Winner: 2016

Didier Deschamps
Winner: 2000

Brian Laudrup
Winner: 1992

AWESOME AWARDS

While all 24 teams at UEFA EURO 2020 are contesting to lift the Henri Delaunay trophy, eyes will also be on other glittering prizes and honours on offer at this summer's festival of football. These include awesome accolades for the highest goal tally, great team play and standout individual performances.

BELOW: Captain Cristiano Ronaldo salutes fans after Portugal win EURO 2016.

OPPOSITE BOTTOM: Portugal hotshot Renato Sanches scores in a penalty shoot-out at EURO 2016.

RIGHT: England striker Harry Kane in action in a EURO 2020 qualifying match against the Czech Republic.

SUPER SCORER

The player who scores the most goals at the tournament will win the Top Scorer Award. It is a prize that top strikers, such as England's Harry Kane, Spain's Álvaro Morata and Poland's Robert Lewandowski, will definitely have their eyes on. With six strikes, France goal machine Antoine Griezmann was top scorer at UEFA EURO 2016.

AWESOME YOUNGSTER

UEFA's technical experts will be watching the top young players in action this summer. High class performances by players born on or after 1 January 1999 can put them in line to scoop up the UEFA Young Player Award. Portugal star Renato Sanches (below) took the trophy in 2016.

SHINING STAR

The player who is considered the competition's best performer will earn the Player of the Tournament award. Players who score lots of goals, keep clean sheets, influence matches or demonstrate superb leadership will be in the running for this brilliant award. Pre-tournament favourites include, among others, Belgium's Eden Hazard and France's Paul Pogba.

TEAM TALK

Who will make the official EURO 2020 Team of the Tournament? The competition's best 11 players, in a formation to be chosen by a panel of judges, will be awarded a spot in the top line-up. Most impressively, Portugal had four stars in the top XI at EURO 2016.

MEGA MATCH

Do not forget that after each EURO game, an official man of the match award is handed out. Seven players, including Cristiano Ronaldo and Antoine Griezmann, won it twice at EURO 2016 and they could grab them again in this summer's tournament.

GROUP A
TURKEY

Tenacious Turkey target a last-eight spot!

The Crescent-Stars sealed their UEFA EURO 2020 spot in 2019 following a tense goalless draw against Iceland. Built on a strong defensive unit, Turkey's firepower lies with forward Cenk Tosun and veteran Burak Yılmaz, while defender Kaan Ayhan poses a danger when he pops up in the box. AC Milan's Hakan Çalhanoğlu is a threat out wide or playing centrally as part of a three-pronged attacking midfield, and his delivery from free-kicks and corners is crucial. Turkey will make it very difficult for opponents to break them down, and could cause problems with sharp counterattacks.

1996

The year Turkey first reached the EURO finals. In 2020, they will be playing in their fifth European Championship.

BELOW: Turkey pose for a team photo in the EURO 2020 qualifiers.

RIGHT: Captain Burak Yılmaz is Turkey's most experienced player.

TEAM GUIDE
CAPTAIN: Burak Yılmaz
COACH: Şenol Güneş
ROUTE TO UEFA EURO 2020: Group H runners-up
PREVIOUS APPEARANCES: 4
BEST FINISH: Semi-finals 2008

WATCH OUT FOR...
CENK TOSUN: Reliable goal scorer
ÇAĞLAR SÖYÜNCÜ: Exciting young defender
HAKAN ÇALHANOĞLU: Excellent passer and free-kick specialist

ITALY

The *Azzurri* are hoping to reach their fourth EURO final!

After failing to qualify for the 2018 FIFA World Cup, Italy are on a mission to prove they have returned to their best. The *Azzurri* were runners-up at both EURO 2012 and 2000, though many players in the current squad are taking part in their first major international tournament. Goal scorers Immobile, Lorenzo Insigne and Andrea Belotti all hit the net in qualifying and look sharp. In notching up a 100 per cent record in qualifying, the Italians have already shown a tough team spirit too – they came from behind to beat both Bosnia and Herzegovina and Armenia in their group.

9

Italy recorded one of the biggest wins in their history as they completed their successful Euro 2020 qualifying campaign by thrashing Armenia 9-1.

TEAM GUIDE

CAPTAIN: Giorgio Chiellini
COACH: Roberto Mancini
ROUTE TO UEFA EURO 2020: Group J winners
PREVIOUS APPEARANCES: 9
BEST FINISH: Champions 1968

WATCH OUT FOR...

ANDREA BELOTTI: Hardworking striker
JORGINHO: Midfielder who can dictate the tempo of play
GIANLUIGI DONNARUMMA: Commanding young keeper

RIGHT: Emerson plays primarily as a left-back, but can also operate as a left-winger.

BELOW: Italy line up against Bosnia and Herzegovina in the EURO 2020 qualifiers.

GROUP A
WALES

The Welsh Dragons are primed to spring another surprise this summer!

After storming their way to the semi-finals at UEFA EURO 2016 (Wales' first appearance at a EURO final tournament), the team are again hoping to cause more upsets at this summer's competition. A lot will be expected of top-class duo Gareth Bale and Aaron Ramsey, but the likes of Daniel James, Joe Allen and the emerging Kieffer Moore will play a big role too. Coach Ryan Giggs played at the highest level for Manchester United and will enjoy leading his country into a major tournament.

TEAM GUIDE
CAPTAIN: Gareth Bale
COACH: Ryan Giggs
ROUTE TO UEFA EURO 2020: Group E runners-up
PREVIOUS APPEARANCES: 1
BEST FINISH: Semi-finals 2016

WATCH OUT FOR...
AARON RAMSEY: Central midfielder with an eye for goal
GARETH BALE: World-class finisher
DANIEL JAMES: Speedy and skilful winger

BELOW: Superstar striker Gareth Bale (bottom row, third from left) spearheads the Welsh attack.

LEFT: Joe Allen has the ability to dictate the tempo of play in midfield.

1
The number of EURO 2020 qualifying matches in which Bale and Ramsey started together – the vital 2-0 win over Hungary.

CYMRU V CROATIA
13 HYDREF 2019 - STADIWM DINAS CAERDYDD

22

SWITZERLAND

The *Schweizer Nati* is packed with flair players in midfield!

Switzerland's teamwork is arguably their biggest strength, which has seen several players scoring in the UEFA EURO 2020 qualifiers to secure their place as Group D winners. Premier League pair Granit Xhaka and Xherdan Shaqiri have more than 160 caps between them and form a vital force in midfield, with Denis Zakaria and Cedric Itten emerging as exciting young players. Zakaria played in all eight games and is a powerful figure in midfield in front of the back three, covering lots of ground and influencing play with his passing and tackling skills.

15

The number of different players who scored for Switzerland during their eight EURO 2020 qualifying matches.

TEAM GUIDE

CAPTAIN: Granit Xhaka
COACH: Vladimir Petković
ROUTE TO UEFA EURO 2020: Group D winners
PREVIOUS APPEARANCES: 4
BEST FINISH: Round of 16 2016

WATCH OUT FOR...

GRANIT XHAKA: Driving force in midfield
XHERDAN SHAQIRI: Creative goalscoring midfielder
CEDRIC ITTEN: Breakthrough striker in the qualifiers

RIGHT: Defensive midfielder Denis Zakaria gives the Swiss backline extra solidity.

BELOW: Switzerland team photo before they faced Denmark in the qualifiers in 2019.

GROUP B
DENMARK

The Danes' defence must be strong to reach the final stages.

Denmark relied on their well-drilled defence and the magic of playmaker Christian Eriksen to secure their place at UEFA EURO 2020. A tense 1-1 draw against the Republic of Ireland saw the Danes earn their spot in the finals, though most impressively they conceded only six goals during the qualifiers. Forwards Martin Braithwaite, Kasper Dolberg, Yussuf Poulsen and Christian Gytkjær – who was a prolific marksman playing for his former club Lech Poznań in Poland – will be hoping to chip in with goals this summer.

TEAM GUIDE
CAPTAIN: Simon Kjær
COACH: Kasper Hjulmand
ROUTE TO UEFA EURO 2020: Group D runners-up
PREVIOUS APPEARANCES: 8
BEST FINISH: Winners 1992

WATCH OUT FOR...
CHRISTIAN ERIKSEN: Creative right-footed midfielder
KASPER SCHMEICHEL: Dominant presence in goal
SIMON KJÆR: Key player in the heart of the defence

29
The number of years ago that Kasper Schmeichel's dad, Peter, helped Denmark win EURO '92.

LEFT: Forward Martin Braithwaite can also play as a winger.

BELOW: Classy defender Simon Kjær (top row, second from right) captains Denmark.

GROUP B
FINLAND

The tournament's newcomers are looking to land a knockout blow this summer!

Despite having never played in a UEFA European Championship, Finland performed superbly in the qualifiers and earned their right to brush shoulders with Europe's mightiest teams this summer. They are looking to repeat what Iceland, their Nordic rivals, did four years ago and make it a debut to remember. Teemu Pukki is Finland's key striker who scored an impressive 10 of Finland's 16 goals in the qualifiers. During the 2020 qualifying campaign, young midfielder Fredrik Jensen also scored twice in his first three matches and imposing keeper Lukáš Hrádecký kept six clean sheets as part of a tough-looking backline.

34

In the history of the UEFA European Championship, Finland are the 34th national team to reach the EURO finals.

BELOW: Finland take part in the EURO finals for the first time this summer.

TEAM GUIDE
CAPTAIN: Tim Sparv
COACH: Markku Kanerva
ROUTE TO UEFA EURO 2020: Group J runners-up
PREVIOUS APPEARANCES: 0
BEST FINISH: Debut

WATCH OUT FOR...
TEEMU PUKKI: Classy finisher
FREDRIK JENSEN: Attacking threat
LUKÁŠ HRÁDECKÝ: Commanding keeper

LEFT: Defensive midfielder and captain Tim Sparv gives his team shape and discipline.

GROUP B
BELGIUM

The Red Devils are among the top sides competing in this summer's tournament!

With goalscorers and creative players such as Eden Hazard, Kevin De Bruyne, Romelu Lukaku and Michy Batshuayi in their side, Belgium pose a threat to any international side they play! The backbone of this exciting team has been together for many years, making Belgium a favourite to pick up the Henri Delaunay Cup on 11 July. The Red Devils won all 10 matches during the qualifiers, scoring a staggering 40 goals and conceded just three, showing what a top-class outfit they are from front to back. It's no secret that fans around the world enjoy watching Belgium in action because of their free-flowing and attack-minded style of play.

S

Belgium became the first team to qualify for UEFA EURO 2020 after beating San Marino 9-0 on 10 October 2019.

BELOW: Belgium are captained by the team's star player Eden Hazard (bottom row, far right).

TEAM GUIDE
CAPTAIN: Eden Hazard
COACH: Roberto Martínez
ROUTE TO UEFA EURO 2020: Group I winners
PREVIOUS APPEARANCES: 5
BEST FINISH: Runners-up 1980

WATCH OUT FOR...
DRIES MERTENS: Experienced forward with clever feet
DIVOCK ORIGI: Impact player from the bench
JAN VERTONGHEN: A key defender who is also a threat in the opposition box

RIGHT: Centre-back Toby Alderweireld brings experience to Belgium's defence.

RUSSIA

The National Team are strong and disciplined!

The 2018 FIFA World Cup saw Russia stage some great performances to beat Saudi Arabia, Egypt and Spain on their way to the quarter-finals. This summer, they hope to pit their talents against Europe's top teams. In qualifying they sealed second spot behind Belgium, scoring 33 goals and conceding just eight. With Igor Akinfeev retired, the prolific goalscorer Artem Dzyuba wears the captain's armband for the first time at a major tournament. His nine goals in qualifying were crucial to the team's progress and in the competition he'll be a threat in and around the penalty box. Russia also have midfielders Aleksandr Golovin and Denis Cheryshev who can break forward in quick counter-attacking moves.

TEAM GUIDE

CAPTAIN: Artem Dzyuba
COACH: Stanislav Cherchesov
ROUTE TO UEFA EURO 2020: Group I runners-up
PREVIOUS APPEARANCES: 11 (6 as USSR)
BEST FINISH: Champions 1960 (as USSR)

WATCH OUT FOR...

ALEKSANDR GOLOVIN: Classy midfielder who supports the strikers
GEORGI DZHIKIYA: Marshalls the defensive line
DENIS CHERYSHEV: Winger with a lethal left foot

LEFT: Russia's captain Artem Dzyuba also spearheads his team's attack.

5

Russia's appearance at EURO 2020 marks the first time the team have reached five UEFA European Championships in a row.

BELOW: Russia line up before playing Cyprus in the EURO 2020 qualifiers.

NETHERLANDS

The classy Dutch return to the big stage!

Even with a talented squad, the Netherlands missed out on playing at both UEFA EURO 2016 and the 2018 FIFA World Cup. However, with Frank de Boer now in charge after the great work Ronald Koeman did before he joined Barcelona, the *Oranje* are much improved, a side that can defend solidly and then spring quickfire counterattacks. Memphis Depay, Ryan Babel, Georginio Wijnaldum, Frenkie de Jong and Luuk de Jong form the team's creative and goalscoring hub, while captain Virgil van Dijk is at the heart of a strong back line.

4

The number of goals the Netherlands scored in the second half to beat Germany 4-2 in a EURO 2020 qualifying match.

BELOW: The Netherlands team photo before their match against Northern Ireland in the EURO 2020 qualifiers.

TEAM GUIDE

CAPTAIN: Virgil van Dijk
COACH: Frank de Boer
ROUTE TO UEFA EURO 2020: Group C runners-up
PREVIOUS APPEARANCES: 9
BEST FINISH: Winners 1988

WATCH OUT FOR...

GEORGINIO WIJNALDUM: Midfielder with a sharp eye for goal
RYAN BABEL: Counterattacking star who loves to assist
MATTHIJS DE LIGT: Forms a formidable defensive partnership with Virgil van Dijk

RIGHT: Forward Memphis Depay can be lethal from free-kicks.

GROUP C
UKRAINE

The Blue and Yellows qualified in style!

In this tournament, Ukraine appear to be a stronger team than they were at UEFA EURO 2016 and 2012. With creative players like Yevhen Konoplyanka supported by the defensive midfielder Taras Stepanenko, they have the talent to progress beyond the group stage for the first time. The attacking duo Andriy Yarmolenko and Oleksandr Zinchenko will be crucial to their success. Usually a defender for his club Manchester City, Zinchenko operates in central midfield on the international stage and was among the scorers in the qualifiers.

TEAM GUIDE
CAPTAIN: Andriy Pyatov
COACH: Andriy Shevchenko
ROUTE TO UEFA EURO 2020: Group B winners
PREVIOUS APPEARANCES: 2
BEST FINISH: Group stage

WATCH OUT FOR...
ANDRIY YARMOLENKO: Awesome left-sided forward
OLEKSANDR ZINCHENKO: Able to play in either defence or attack
YEVHEN KONOPLYANKA: Midfielder with an eye for goal

FAR LEFT: Ukraine pose for a group picture before a EURO 2020 Group B qualifier match.

LEFT: Goalkeeper and captain Andriy Pyatov marshals his team from the back.

19
Midfielder Oleksandr Zinchenko is Ukraine's youngest scorer. He was 19 years and 214 days old when he netted his first international goal.

29

AUSTRIA

The boys in red are aiming to beat the big teams at UEFA EURO 2020!

Austria are looking to improve on their performances at both EURO 2016 and EURO 2008 (their only two outings in the competition) by recording their first win at the tournament. Franco Foda's team have every chance, having looked strong in qualifying as Group G runners-up, despite starting the campaign with defeats by both Poland and Israel. Marko Arnautović is Austria's main threat in attack, backed up by the skills and goals of Marcel Sabitzer after his impressive season for RB Leipzig in Germany's Bundesliga. The defence is marshalled by the tough duo of Aleksandar Dragović and Martin Hinteregger.

TEAM GUIDE

CAPTAIN: Julian Baumgartlinger
COACH: Franco Foda
ROUTE TO UEFA EURO 2020: Group G runners-up
PREVIOUS APPEARANCES: 2
BEST FINISH: Group stage

WATCH OUT FOR...

MARCEL SABITZER: Skilful midfielder or forward
DAVID ALABA: Versatile left-footed star
MARKO ARNAUTOVIĆ: Powerful and technical striker

RIGHT: Austria captain Julian Baumgartlinger played a key role in the EURO 2020 qualifiers.

7

Star striker Marko Arnautović wears the No7 shirt for Austria. He also wears the same number for his club, Shanghai SIPG.

BELOW: Austria team photo before their EURO 2020 qualifying match v Slovenia.

NORTH MACEDONIA

Exciting times as the newcomers target the knockout stage!

When Goran Pandev slotted the ball home for a 1-0 win over Georgia in November, it sealed North Macedonia's first appearance at a major tournament. Igor Angelovski's team were in fine form ahead of that famous play-off final win and were unbeaten in six games thanks to their tough defence and impressive team spirit. Leeds United's Ezgjan Alioski remains a driving force from midfield and Aleksandar Trajkovski will support Pandev with his runs into the box. What North Macedonia lack in EURO experience they will aim to make up for with heaps of enthusiasm, energy and hard work.

36

Captain Goran Pandev is the country's record scorer, netting 36 goals in 114 games since 2001.

TEAM GUIDE

CAPTAIN: Goran Pandev
COACH: Igor Angelovski
ROUTE TO UEFA EURO 2020: UEFA Nations League, Path D play-off final winners
PREVIOUS APPEARANCES: 0
BEST FINISH: Debut

WATCH OUT FOR...

ELJIF ELMAS: Young playmaker with great vision
EZGJAN ALIOSKI: Energetic and creative
ALEKSANDAR TRAJKOVSKI: Dangerous right foot around the box

RIGHT: Captain Goran Pandev will lead North Macedonia's attack at EURO 2020.

ABOVE: North Macedonia line up for a team photo ahead of their EURO 2020 qualifier match against Armenia.

GROUP D
ENGLAND

The Three Lions are roaring for glory!

England have looked impressive in qualifying for recent tournaments and once again they topped their group. The Three Lions have a strong team, packed with Premier League stars who are capable of testing the best defences. Harry Kane, Raheem Sterling and Marcus Rashford form a dangerous trio up front, supported by the exciting talent of players such as Jadon Sancho and Mason Mount. Coach Gareth Southgate is not afraid to change his team and system, and with gifted players competing for the full-back spots, including Liverpool's right-back Trent Alexander-Arnold, he has the option of adding extra firepower to England's attacking force. With Wembley staging the UEFA EURO 2020 final, England have a huge incentive to go all the way.

25

England last reached the semi-final stage of the EURO finals 25 years ago in 1996. They eventually lost to Germany in a penalty shoot-out.

BELOW: England line up against the Czech Republic in the EURO 2020 qualifiers.

TEAM GUIDE
CAPTAIN: Harry Kane
COACH: Gareth Southgate
ROUTE TO UEFA EURO 2020: Group A winners
PREVIOUS APPEARANCES: 9
BEST FINISH: Third place 1968

WATCH OUT FOR...
HARRY KANE: Penalty-box predator
RAHEEM STERLING: Goal threat with quick feet
JADON SANCHO: Speedy youngster with silky skills

RIGHT: Forward Marcus Rashford adds pace and power to England's attacking unit.

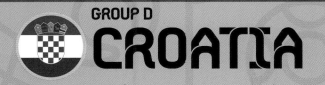

CROATIA

This big-tournament team will fear no one!

Even though they have never reached the semi-final stage of a UEFA European Championship, Croatia will have the confidence to make a big impression this summer. The 2018 FIFA World Cup runners-up have experienced stars such as Luka Modrić, Ivan Perišić and Mateo Kovačić to call upon, plus the skills of their rising star striker Bruno Petković. In qualifying they did not score as heavily as England or Belgium, but the team in the famous red and white checked shirts can be world beaters when they hit top gear at a major tournament.

TEAM GUIDE
CAPTAIN: Luka Modrić
COACH: Zlatko Dalić
ROUTE TO UEFA EURO 2020: Group E winners
PREVIOUS APPEARANCES: 5
BEST FINISH: Quarter-finals 2008 and 1996

WATCH OUT FOR...
LUKA MODRIĆ: World-class playmaker
IVAN PERIŠIĆ: Tricky skills on the wing
BRUNO PETKOVIĆ: Exciting striker

RIGHT: Versatile midfielder Mateo Kovačić gives Croatia many attacking options.

2-1
The result in Croatia's first three EURO 2020 qualifying games. They won two of these games and lost the other.

BELOW: Croatia are led by superstar Luka Modrić (bottom row, far right).

33

GROUP D

SCOTLAND

After 25 years, the Tartan Army qualify for the EURO finals and are keen to impress!

It has been a long wait for Scotland to reach a major tournament, but Steve Clarke's team are excited to be mixing it again with Europe's best. They developed a tough defensive style over the last couple of years, with flair players like Ryan Fraser and John McGinn adding quality to their attack. Lyndon Dykes is a menace up front and watch out for captain Andrew Robertson bursting forward from the back. The rest of Group D will be aware of how hard Scotland battled in their play-off final win in Serbia in November 2020. This spirited team has a superb work ethic and is more than capable of causing one or two upsets.

1996

Scotland's last appearance at the EURO finals was in 1996, a tournament when they also faced England at Wembley.

BELOW: Scotland line up before their match against Serbia in the EURO 2020 play-off final.

TEAM GUIDE
CAPTAIN: Andrew Robertson
COACH: Steve Clarke
ROUTE TO UEFA EURO 2020: UEFA Nations League, Path C play-off final winners
PREVIOUS APPEARANCES: 2
BEST FINISH: Group stage

WATCH OUT FOR...
JOHN MCGINN: Superb passer who controls midfield
ANDREW ROBERTSON: Attacking left-back with great delivery
LYNDON DYKES: Powerful striker poses an aerial threat

RIGHT: Winger Ryan Fraser is a strong and versatile player who can also operate as a right-back.

CZECH REPUBLIC

The experienced football nation have the potential to cause a major upset!

The Czech Republic proved their strength with a 2-1 win over England in the Group A qualifiers (handing the Three Lions their first defeat in a EURO qualifying campaign in 10 years). Patrik Schick, who has experience of playing in Serie A and the Bundesliga, leads their attack. Most notably, he scored a match-winning double against Bulgaria in the qualifiers. Captain Vladimír Darida can take up a forward position in the Czech Republic's favoured 4-2-3-1 system, but is also clever enough to drop deep and control the midfield. Although the Czechs have performed well in past EURO finals, the pain of failing to win a single match at EURO 2016 will spur them on.

7

Since the Czech Republic gained indepedence (after Czechoslovakia split up) in 1993, they have qualified for seven EURO finals in a row.

TEAM GUIDE

CAPTAIN: Vladimír Darida
COACH: Jaroslav Šilhavý
ROUTE TO UEFA EURO 2020: Group A runner-up
PREVIOUS APPEARANCES: 9
BEST FINISH: Winners 1976 (as Czechoslovakia)

WATCH OUT FOR...

VLADIMIR DARIDA: Hardworking midfield leader
TOMÁŠ SOUČEK: Tall midfielder with neat skills
PAVEL KADEŘÁBEK: A class act at right-back

RIGHT: Centre-forward Patrik Schick is well-known for his fierce left-footed strike.

BELOW: The Czech Republic is captained by Vladimír Darida (bottom row, second from left).

GROUP E
SPAIN

La Roja are a team of fierce attacking stars!

With 31 goals in qualifying and no defeats, Spain are rightly seen as one of the tournament favourites. Captain Sergio Ramos has tasted success twice, at UEFA EURO 2012 and 2008, and his defensive qualities make Spain solid at the back. Spain usually dominate possession against even the top sides, but they have to be patient and wait for chances as opposition sides tend to defend deep against them. Coach Luis Enrique probably has the squad with the best strength in depth in the competition and picking the starting XI could be his biggest challenge in the first couple of games.

2
Spain have won the competition twice in the 21st century and are the only country to manage back-to-back wins.

BELOW: Spain line up for a team photo before playing Norway in the EURO 2020 qualifiers.

TEAM GUIDE
CAPTAIN: Sergio Ramos
COACH: Luis Enrique
ROUTE TO UEFA EURO 2020: Group F winners
PREVIOUS APPEARANCES: 10
BEST FINISH: Champions 1964, 2008, 2012

WATCH OUT FOR...
ÁLVARO MORATA: Fast, powerful and a cool finisher
JESÚS NAVAS: Dangerous attacker from right-back
SERGIO BUSQUETS: Protects the defence from midfield

LEFT: Forward Rodrigo was on top goalscoring form during the qualifiers helping Spain top the group.

GROUP E
SWEDEN

Strong qualifying underlines the quality of a team that is improving all the time!

Before Sweden had even secured their UEFA EURO 2020 place in November 2019 with a 2-0 win over Romania, it was clear that the Scandinavians were a team on the rise. Coach Janne Andersson took them to the 2018 FIFA World Cup – their first in 12 years – before guiding them to a UEFA Nations League group position ahead of Russia and Turkey. While the squad may not boast superstar names, determined players such as Robin Olsen, Victor Lindelöf and Sebastian Larsson will make them tough opponents.

17
Alexander Isak was just 17 years old when he scored his first goal for Sweden in 2017.

BELOW: Sweden line up for a team photo before facing Spain in the EURO 2020 qualifiers.

TEAM GUIDE
CAPTAIN: Andreas Granqvist
COACH: Janne Andersson
ROUTE TO UEFA EURO 2020: Group F runners-up
PREVIOUS APPEARANCES: 6
BEST FINISH: Semi-finals 1992

WATCH OUT FOR...
ROBIN QUAISON: Top scorer in qualifying
ALEXANDER ISAK: Impactful young striker
ROBIN OLSEN: Keeper full of confidence

RIGHT: Defender Victor Lindelöf can be an attacking threat with his accurate long passes.

POLAND

The Eagles are led by a superstar captain!

By winning the first four games in the qualifying stage of EURO 2020, Poland all but booked a place in their fourth UEFA European Championship in a row. Spearheaded by the striking duo of Robert Lewandowski and Krzysztof Piątek, Poland's squad is loaded with tournament experience. Arkadiusz Milik became a big name scoring goals for Napoli in the 2019-20 season while tenacious winger Kamil Grosicki can pick a clever pass too. Poland's success at EURO 2020 depends on captain Lewandowski, who can perform magic from anywhere on the pitch. Can he take Poland beyond the quarter-finals this summer?

2

Substitutes scored both goals in Poland's 2-0 win over North Macedonia in the qualifiers, sealing Poland's place at EURO 2020.

TEAM GUIDE

CAPTAIN: Robert Lewandowski
COACH: Paolo Sousa
ROUTE TO UEFA EURO 2020: Group G winners
PREVIOUS APPEARANCES: 3
BEST FINISH: Quarter-finals 2016

WATCH OUT FOR...

KRZYSZTOF PIĄTEK: Dangerous striker
KAMIL GLICK: Leader in defence
ROBERT LEWANDOWSKI: World-class goalscorer

RIGHT: Experienced winger Kamil Grosicki played in both EURO 2012 and 2016.

BELOW: Robert Lewandowski (bottom row, third from left) captains the Poland team.

SLOVAKIA

The Falcons are determined to at least match their performance at EURO 2016!

Slovakia broke the hearts of Northern Ireland fans in their play-off final, scoring in extra time to book a place at UEFA EURO 2020. In their qualifying group, Slovakia beat Hungary twice and drew with Wales – two teams who also reached the finals – so they should not be seen as easy targets after reaching the finals through the play-offs in November. They rely greatly on the creativity and leadership of midfield captain Marek Hamšík, and with popular defender Martin Škrtel now retired, their defence is well marshalled by Internazionale's Milan Škriniar.

22

Marek Hamšík captained Slovakia at the 2010 FIFA World Cup at the age of just 22.

RIGHT:-Captain Marek Hamšík is Slovakia's heartbeat and their main attacking threat.

TEAM GUIDE
CAPTAIN: Marek Hamšík
COACH: Štefan Tarkovič
ROUTE TO UEFA EURO 2020: UEFA Nations League, Path B play-off final winners
PREVIOUS APPEARANCES: 1
BEST FINISH: Round of 16 2016

WATCH OUT FOR...
RÓBERT MAK: Hardworking right winger
MILAN ŠKRINIAR: Strong tackler who is quick to make clearances
RÓBERT BOŽENÍK: Talented forward who scored three qualifying goals

BELOW: Slovakia pose for a team photo ahead of their EURO 2020 qualifier match against Wales in 2019.

GROUP F
HUNGARY

The *Magyars* are ready to cause an upset in a group packed with talented teams!

Germany, Portugal and France will need to watch Hungary very closely for the full 90 minutes in Group F. Marco Rossi's team staged an amazing late comeback against Iceland in the play-off final in November, scoring in the 88th and 92nd minute to claim a 2-1 victory and their place this summer. Their three group opponents may all have world-class talents, but Hungary have some stars of their own and will hope that 21-year-old Dominik Szoboszlai shines on the biggest stage.

Playing their first two group games at the impressive new Puskas Arena in Budapest will really inspire Hungary.

2
This is the first time Hungary have qualified for two EURO finals in a row, after they reached the round of 16 at UEFA EURO 2016.

TEAM GUIDE
CAPTAIN: Ádám Szalai
COACH: Marco Rossi
ROUTE TO UEFA EURO 2020: UEFA Nations League, Path A play-off final winners
PREVIOUS APPEARANCES: 3
BEST FINISH: Third 1964

WATCH OUT FOR...
WILLI ORBÁN: Strong and organised centre-back
DOMINIK SZOBOSZLAI: Exciting young midfielder with an eye for goal
PÉTER GULÁCSI: Reliable goalkeeper who commands his area

LEFT: Forward and captain Ádám Szalai is Hungary's most experienced player.

ABOVE: Hungary line up ahead of their EURO 2020 qualifier match against Croatia in 2019.

40

PORTUGAL

The champions challenge again for the cup!

Having lifted the trophy at UEFA EURO 2016, Cristiano Ronaldo's team is targeting the top prize once more. Although now 36, Ronaldo still shows no sign of slowing and performed at top level in 2019, blasting 14 goals in just 10 international appearances. Fans also have the joy of watching playmakers like Bernardo Silva, William Carvalho and João Moutinho in action, as well as the rising young superstar, João Félix, who has the flair and vision to influence games up front. The squad may not be filled with as many star players as that of Spain, France or Belgium, but Portugal still have the talent and belief to reach their third final this century.

101

Portugal superstar forward Cristiano Ronaldo scored his 101st international goal in September 2020.

TEAM GUIDE
CAPTAIN: Cristiano Ronaldo
COACH: Fernando Santos
ROUTE TO UEFA EURO 2020: Group B runners up
PREVIOUS APPEARANCES: 7
BEST FINISH: Champions 2016

WATCH OUT FOR...
BERNARDO SILVA: Clever and creative midfielder
JOÃO FÉLIX: Talented young forward
CRISTIANO RONALDO: World-class striker

LEFT: João Moutinho forms the midfield backbone of the Portugal team.

BOTTOM LEFT: Portugal are led by world-class striker Cristiano Ronaldo (top row, far right).

GROUP F

FRANCE

Les Bleus **have the pedigree to win their third European title!**

Opposition defenders at EURO 2020 will fear France's firepower that includes the likes of Kylian Mbappé, Antoine Griezmann, Kingsley Coman and Olivier Giroud. Apart from Bayern Munich winger Coman, the others helped France win the 2018 FIFA World Cup and are now intent on helping *Les Bleus* win their second major title in three years and get over the blow of losing the UEFA EURO 2016 final to Portugal. France have the necessary winning spirit in coach Didier Deschamps as well as the squad to take the title again. Superstar striker Mbappé, still only 22, could be the player of the tournament.

TEAM GUIDE
CAPTAIN: Hugo Lloris
COACH: Didier Deschamps
ROUTE TO UEFA EURO 2020: Group H winners
PREVIOUS APPEARANCES: 9
BEST FINISH: Champions 1984, 2000

WATCH OUT FOR...
ANTOINE GRIEZMANN: Big threat around the box
KINGSLEY COMAN: Pace and energy in attack
RAPHAËL VARANE: Cool on the ball at the back

LEFT: Striker Olivier Giroud is known for his effective hold-up play and is a potent aerial threat.

BELOW: France team photo before their match against Albania in the 2020 qualifiers.

21
The current coach of France, Didier Deschamps, captained the national side to the European title 21 years ago.

42

GROUP F
GERMANY

Die Mannschaft seek their fourth EURO title!

Usually dominant during qualification, Germany finished top of their qualifying group for UEFA EURO 2020. They relied on a 90th-minute winner in the Netherlands and actually lost 4-2 at home to the Dutch, before victory in Northern Ireland got them back on track. Nevertheless, Germany are a true giant in world football, and will count on the experience of captain Manuel Neuer to marshal them through the competition. What's more, with exciting young goal scorers like Timo Werner, Serge Gnabry and Leroy Sané they promise to entertain this summer. As always, you can never write off *Die Mannschaft* in a major competition.

TEAM GUIDE
CAPTAIN: Manuel Neuer
COACH: Joachim Löw
ROUTE TO UEFA EURO 2020: Group C winners
PREVIOUS APPEARANCES: 12
BEST FINISH: Champions 1972*, 1980*, 1996
(*as West Germany)

WATCH OUT FOR...
TONI KROOS: Dominating midfielder who has a fierce shot
SERGE GNABRY: Striker with a top international record
MANUEL NEUER: Commanding keeper and captain

RIGHT: Marco Reus is a versatile attacker with a powerful finish.

ABOVE: Germany specialise in hitting their best form at major tournaments.

15
Joachim Löw has managed Germany for more than 15 years. EURO 2020 is Löw's fourth appearance at a EURO finals tournamant as Germany's coach.

43

UEFA EURO 2020 STARS: FORWARDS

It is time to reveal the players set to light up UEFA EURO 2020! Here is a selection of the sharpest shooters featuring in this summer's football extravaganza!

HARRY KANE

COUNTRY: England
CLUB: Tottenham Hotspur (England)
BORN: 28 July 1993
GAMES: 51
GOALS: 32

Harry Kane captained England through the UEFA EURO 2020 qualifiers, blasting 12 goals in eight games, including a hat-trick against Bulgaria. England's first-choice frontman has the strength and experience to play as a lone central striker, though he is more effective with Raheem Sterling making lively runs around him. Kane can score all sorts of goals with either foot, from long-range efforts to well-placed headers as well as tap-ins inside the six-yard box. He is a superb penalty-taker too, with four of his qualifying goals coming from the spot. With Kane on the pitch the Three Lions will always be a force.

HARRY KANE QUIZ

QUESTION 1: Against which team did Kane score a hat-trick during the UEFA EURO 2020 qualifiers?

A. **Czech Republic** ☑   B. **Montenegro** ☑   C. **Bulgaria** ☑

QUESTION 2: In which year was Kane appointed England captain?

A. **2016** ☑   B. **2017** ☑   C. **2018** ☑

QUESTION 3: How long did it take Kane to score his first international goal after making his England debut?

A. **80 seconds** ☑   B. **95 seconds** ☑   C. **120 seconds** ☑

The **answers** are on **page 59**

44

ROMELU LUKAKU

COUNTRY: Belgium
CLUB: Internazionale (Italy)
BORN: 13 May 1993
GAMES: 89
GOALS: 57

During the EURO 2020 qualifiers, Romelu Lukaku was on sparkling form and, ably supported by Eden Hazard, Kevin De Bruyne and Dries Mertens, helped Belgium become the first side to qualify for this summer's tournament. The muscular striker has always been a hit on the international stage and is already the country's all-time top goalscorer with more than 50 goals, which includes the seven goals he netted in qualifying Group I. If Lukaku brings his recent international form to UEFA EURO 2020, there's every chance his name could be on the Top Scorer Award for leading the goal tally this summer!

KYLIAN MBAPPÉ

COUNTRY: France
CLUB: Paris Saint-Germain (France)
BORN: 20 December 1998
GAMES: 33
GOALS: 13

Speed, power, tricks, vision – France superstar Kylian Mbappé has them all! Alongside Antoine Griezmann and Olivier Giroud, the Paris Saint-Germain star leads the attack for the current FIFA World Cup champions and he is ready to shine in his first UEFA European Championship. Playing club football with Neymar at Paris has made Mbappé into a more fearsome goalscorer, and many fans say it has taken his game to another level since his move to the capital. Mbappé can play as a central striker or drift out wide and dribble into the box. Defenders must deny him space otherwise he is sure to seize any attacking opportunity.

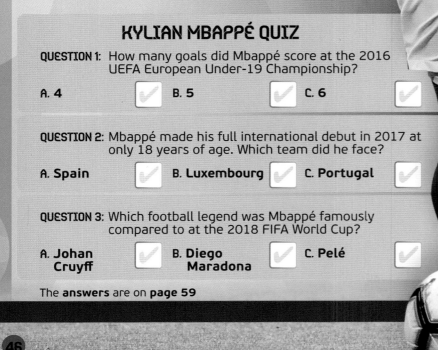

KYLIAN MBAPPÉ QUIZ

QUESTION 1: How many goals did Mbappé score at the 2016 UEFA European Under-19 Championship?

A. 4 ☑ B. 5 ☑ C. 6 ☑

QUESTION 2: Mbappé made his full international debut in 2017 at only 18 years of age. Which team did he face?

A. Spain ☑ B. Luxembourg ☑ C. Portugal ☑

QUESTION 3: Which football legend was Mbappé famously compared to at the 2018 FIFA World Cup?

A. Johan Cruyff ☑ B. Diego Maradona ☑ C. Pelé ☑

The **answers** are on **page 59**

ÁLVARO MORATA

COUNTRY: Spain
CLUB: Juventus (Italy, on loan from Real Madrid)
BORN: 23 October 1992
GAMES: 36
GOALS: 18

Up against the likes of Mikel Oyarzabal and Rodrigo for a spot in Spain's awesome attack. Alvaro Morata must use all of his speed, skill and experience to earn his place in the team and cause chaos for Europe's top defenders. The former Chelsea and Real Madrid striker scored four goals in the UEFA EURO 2020 qualifiers, including a match-winning double in Malta, to boost his chances of making the starting line up when Spain kick off their campaign this summer. Morata works hard for *La Roja* and his power in the air gives Spain a useful option from free-kicks, corners and crosses into the box.

UEFA EURO 2020 STARS:
MIDFIELDERS

The best teams usually include the most creative playmakers in midfield. Check out these stars who will be showcasing their skills at UEFA EURO 2020.

EDEN HAZARD

COUNTRY: Belgium
CLUB: Real Madrid (Spain)
BORN: 7 January 1991
GAMES: 106
GOALS: 32

Belgium's ace midfielder Eden Hazard is often unstoppable on the pitch. Drifting between midfield and attack, charging through the centre or cutting in from the wing at speed, Hazard makes the ball stick to his feet like glue. He leads a star-studded Belgium team, and playing alongside Kevin De Bruyne, the pair forms a creative duo that is among the best on the planet. Hazard has a fine international goal tally too, scoring a goal in every three games. If Hazard hits top gear, Belgium could easily take the UEFA EURO 2020 title on 11 July.

EDEN HAZARD QUIZ

QUESTION 1: Against which team did Hazard score his first international goal in 2011?

A. Turkey ☑   B. Azerbaijan ☑   C. Kazakhstan ☑

QUESTION 2: Which player did Hazard replace as Belgium captain in 2015?

A. Vincent Kompany ☑   B. Dries Mertens ☑   C. Thomas Vermaelen ☑

QUESTION 3: Name the player Hazard idolised growing up.

A. Jan Ceulemans ☑   B. Zinédine Zidane ☑   C. Ronaldinho ☑

The **answers** are on **page 59**

MARCO VERRATTI

COUNTRY: Italy
CLUB: Paris Saint-Germain (France)
BORN: 5 November 1992
GAMES: 38
GOALS: 3

A key part of Italy's revival and smooth progress through UEFA EURO 2020 qualifying has been the form of Marco Verratti (who missed UEFA EURO 2016 through injury). As the link between defence and attack, Verratti can pass, tackle, dribble and press the opposition, making the difficult things look simple. What's more, having been a Paris Saint-Germain player for the past nine seasons, Verratti brings big-game experience to the national side. The *Azzurri* will rely on his vision and composure this summer to help steer them beyond the group stage and perhaps take them to the final.

PAUL POGBA

COUNTRY: France
CLUB: Manchester United (England)
BORN: 15 March 1993
GAMES: 75
GOALS: 10

To be a highly regarded midfielder for a successful European team you need to have energy, a physical presence, agile footwork, a quick brain and goals to your name. Luckily for France, Paul Pogba has all of these skills that come to the fore in the big games. UEFA EURO 2020 will be the fourth major international tournament the Manchester United man has played in and he's keen to add a winners' medal to the runners-up prize he took home from UEFA EURO 2016. Don't be surprised to see his name on the scoresheet this summer.

PAUL POGBA QUIZ

QUESTION 1: What nickname did Pogba earn while he was a player at Juventus?

A. **Il Polpo** ☑   B. **Il Vento** ☑   C. **Il Premio** ☑

QUESTION 2: Pogba has two older twin brothers who are also footballers, but what country do they play for?

A. **Ghana** ☑   B. **Guinea** ☑   C. **Gabon** ☑

QUESTION 3: In what year was Pogba shortlisted for the UEFA Men's Player of the Year award?

A. **2015** ☑   B. **2016** ☑   C. **2017** ☑

The **answers** are on **page 59**

TONI KROOS

COUNTRY: Germany
CLUB: Real Madrid (Spain)
BORN: 4 January 1990
GAMES: 101
GOALS: 17

You do not win the trophies that Germany's master midfielder has without being an exceptional talent. Even though he is only 31, Kroos has picked up more than 20 major honours for club and country, including four UEFA Champions Leagues and the 2014 FIFA World Cup. Joachim Löw's squad has seen many changes over the last few years, but Kroos's epic assists, passing and shooting skills mean that Germany just can't leave him out. He's also the experienced head among younger midfielders like Kai Havertz and Leon Goretzka.

UEFA EURO 2020 STARS:
DEFENDERS

All teams at UEFA EURO 2020 will undoubtedly need a rock-solid defence if they are to win the title. Here are some of the toughest defenders featuring this summer.

™

JOÃO CANCELO

COUNTRY: Portugal
CLUB: Manchester City (England)
BORN: 27 May 1994
GAMES: 22
GOALS: 4

Right-back João Cancelo is so talented that he can also play as a left-back or on either wing! Not only is he fast and skilful going forward but is also a brilliant tackler. Cancelo represented Portugal in the 2012 UEFA European Under-19 Championship and was a squad member of the team that won the 2019 UEFA Nations League title. He may not yet be a famous name on the international scene, but he is more than capable of mixing it with the best players at the EURO finals this summer.

VIRGIL VAN DIJK

COUNTRY: Netherlands
CLUB: Liverpool (England)
BORN: 8 July 1991
GAMES: 38
GOALS: 4

Crowned UEFA Men's Player of the Year in 2019 ahead of Cristiano Ronaldo and Lionel Messi, there's no denying Virgil van Dijk's world-class status. The Netherlands captain is a powerful defender, with great heading, tackling and clearing skills. He often starts attacks by launching a clever pass from defence and can also get on the end of set pieces and score with a rocket header. If fit, playing in his first EURO finals, Van Dijk's performances will be a factor in how far the *Oranje* can go this summer.

SERGIO RAMOS

COUNTRY: Spain
CLUB: Real Madrid (Spain)
BORN: 30 March 1986
GAMES: 178
GOALS: 23

It would be easy to write an entire book on the titles Sergio Ramos has won in the game! He is Spain's most famous defender, who has played a record number of matches and is even among the top ten goal scorers for his country. With two EURO titles and a FIFA World Cup title already in his locker, Ramos is a winner and a big-game player. At 35, he still has enough pace, plus a honed positional sense, to snuff out attacks. Ramos will need to keep his discipline, though, as he has collected more than 270 cards in his career.

HARRY MAGUIRE

COUNTRY: England
CLUB: Manchester United (England)
BORN: 5 March 1993
GAMES: 30
GOALS: 2

A key defender for his club Manchester United, Harry Maguire has the power, experience, temperament and cool ball-playing skills to keep even the best strikers quiet during a match. Since the 2018 FIFA World Cup, when England reached the semi-final, Maguire has been a regular name on coach Gareth Southgate's team sheet, forming the backbone of the England defence. Maguire is also effective at making great passes from defence and is always a threat in the oppositon's box from free-kicks and corners.

UEFA EURO 2020 STARS: GOALKEEPERS

Check out a selection of the top shot stoppers who will be looking to guide their teams to European glory at this summer's competition.

JORDAN PICKFORD

COUNTRY: England
CLUB: Everton (England)
BORN: 7 March 1994
GAMES: 30
DEBUT: 2017

Although perhaps not as tall as other top international keepers, England's Jordan Pickford nevertheless commands his box with powerful displays. The Everton goalie is a fast-thinking and confident character, not afraid to rush from his line to stop a one-on-one attack or punch the ball clear from a dangerous cross into the box. Among Pickford's best weapons is his ball distribution – he can kick an accurate pass or throw a long ball onto the toe of a team-mate and get a quick counterattack underway.

THIBAUT COURTOIS

COUNTRY: Belgium
CLUB: Real Madrid (Spain)
BORN: 11 May 1992
GAMES: 81
DEBUT: 2011

The big Belgian played in nine of his nation's EURO qualifying matches, letting in just two goals as they cruised through. Courtois uses his quick reflexes to reach almost unstoppable shots. Playing behind one of the world's most exciting international attacking teams means the Real Madrid star must be alert and ready when the ball does enter his box. He was disappointed to only reach the semi-finals at the 2018 FIFA World Cup and a place in this summer's final is very much his target.

MANUEL NEUER

COUNTRY: Germany
CLUB: Bayern Munich (Germany)
BORN: 27 March 1986
GAMES: 96
DEBUT: 2009

As he approaches 100 games for his country and with a FIFA World Cup winner's medal already in his pocket, the Germany captain would love to add the European title to his long list of achievements. The experienced keeper holds off the challenge of Barcelona's Marc-André ter Stegen to keep his place between the posts, using his power, agility and kicking skills to command his box and play out from the back. Neuer rarely puts a glove, or foot, wrong on the pitch.

WOJCIECH SZCZĘSNY

COUNTRY: Poland
CLUB: Juventus (Italy)
BORN: 18 April 1990
GAMES: 49
DEBUT: 2009

Although he has to compete with West Ham's Łukasz Fabiański to play for Poland, Wojciech Szczęsny rises to the challenge and remains in top form for his country. Plus you only get to be the first-choice keeper for Juventus, one of the world's biggest clubs, if you are a world-class talent too! Szczęsny played in six UEFA EURO 2020 qualifiying games, keeping four clean sheets to help steer Poland safely through. He has had a mixed time at previous EURO finals, though, with injury and suspension affecting him in 2012 and 2016. He wants to make up for that this summer.

UEFA EURO 2020 QUIZ: PART 1

Put your footy brain to the test with our quick EURO 2020 quiz! All you have to do is read each question and then fill in your answer(s) in the space provided. As it's the 60th anniversary of the UEFA European Championship, the total score is out of 60.

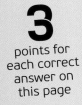

3 points for each correct answer on this page

CAPTAIN FANTASTIC
These incredible captains led their country to success in EURO finals, but in which year?

A

B

C

Theo Zagorakis `2` `0` `?` `?`

Jürgen Klinsmann `1` `9` `?` `?`

Giacinto Facchetti `1` `9` `?` `?`

GREAT EIGHTS
Below are the jerseys of some legendary players who have worn the No8 shirt at EURO finals. Can you fill in the missing letters to complete their names?

ÖZ _ _

A

X _ V _

B

DAVI _ _

C

_ _ _ COIGNE

D

WHEN IN ROME

UEFA EURO 2020 kicks off in the Olimpico in Rome, but which of these two pictures shows that venue?

2 points for each correct answer on this page

KIT CLOSE-UP

The camera has zoomed in on these football shirts worn during UEFA EURO 2020 qualifiers. Which national team does each shirt belong to?

Your answer:

UEFA EURO 2020 QUIZ: PART 2

HAZARD WARNING

Below is a picture of Belgium's Eden Hazard taking on Russia in a UEFA EURO 2020 qualifier. The image beside it has five differences – can you circle them all?

2 points for each correct answer

PAY THE PENALTY

Spain striker Álvaro Morata takes a penalty, but which is the real ball in the picture: A, B, C or D?

5 points for the correct answer

FINAL FINISH

Tick the five players who have scored in a UEFA European Championship final.

VAN BASTEN	TREZEGUET	KANE	TORRES
✓	✓	✓	✓

ÉDER	LEWANDOWSKI	GOMEZ	CHARISTEAS
✓	✓	✓	✓

2 points for each correct answer

GOAL GREATS

These goal stars have scored lots of times at EURO finals, but how many exactly? Match the player to the number of goals from the list.

2 points for each correct answer

Alan Shearer

Zinédine Zidane

Zlatan Ibrahimović

5 GOALS   **S** GOALS   **7** GOALS

MY FINAL SCORE ⬤ / 60?

Answers

PART 1
Captain Fantastic: Theo Zagorakis 2004; Jürgen Klinsmann 1996; Giacinto Facchetti 1968
Great Eights: A. Özil; B. Xavi; C. Davids; D. Gascoigne
When in Rome: A
Kit Close-up: 1. Germany; 2. Italy; 3. England

PART 2
Hazard Warning

Pay The Penalty: B
Final Finish: Van Basten, Trezeguet, Torres, Éder, Charisteas
Goal Greats: Zinédine Zidane 5; Zlatan Ibrahimović 6; Alan Shearer 7

PLAYER QUIZ
Harry Kane: 1C; 2B; 3A
Kylian Mbappé: 1B; 2B; 3C
Eden Hazard: 1C; 2A; 3B
Paul Pogba: 1A; 2B; 3A

READER RECORDS

Watch all the action from UEFA EURO 2020 and write down your favourite games, goals, teams and moments. It is the best way to keep a record of all your personal highlights from this incredible footy event.

UEFA EURO 2020 WINNERS:

RUNNERS-UP:

GOLDEN BOOT WINNER: HE SCORED   GOALS

FAVOURITE TEAM:

I LIKED THAT TEAM BECAUSE:

FAVOURITE PLAYER:

HE WAS THE BEST BECAUSE:

FAVOURITE YOUNG PLAYER:

MOST SKILFUL PLAYER:

BEST TEAM TO WATCH:

MY TEAM OF THE TOURNAMENT:

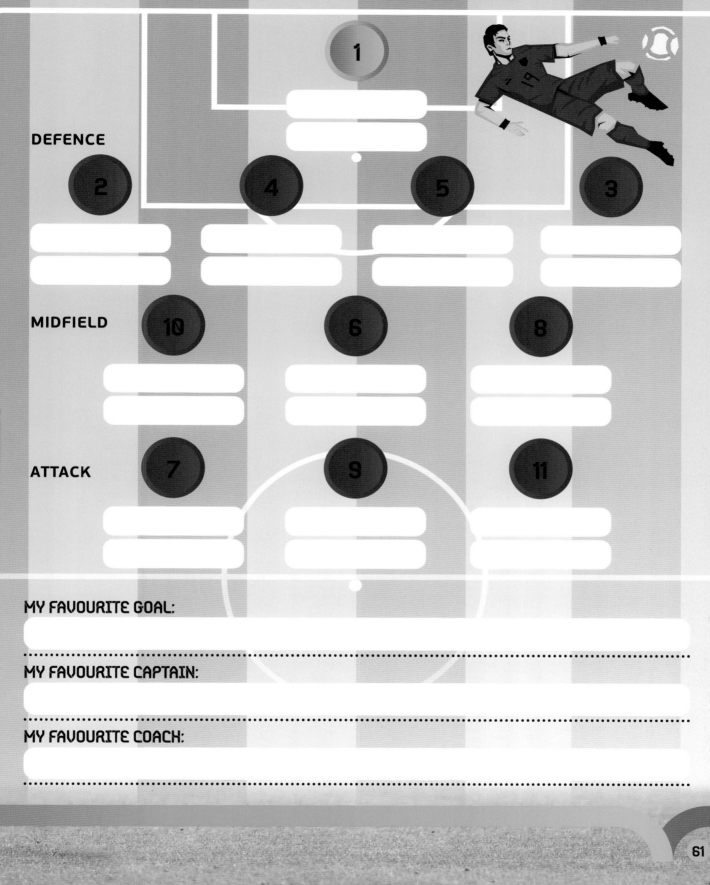

DEFENCE

MIDFIELD

ATTACK

MY FAVOURITE GOAL:

MY FAVOURITE CAPTAIN:

MY FAVOURITE COACH:

MATCH SCHEDULE AND RESULTS CHART

On these pages you can fill in the results from all 51 games at the UEFA EURO 2020 finals around Europe this summer. Do not miss the big kick-off on 11 June, with the final taking place on 11 July. Enjoy!

GROUP A

11 June, 21:00	Turkey	☐ ☐	Italy	Rome
12 June, 15:00	Wales	☐ ☐	Switzerland	Baku
16 June, 18:00	Turkey	☐ ☐	Wales	Baku
16 June, 21:00	Italy	☐ ☐	Switzerland	Rome
20 June, 18:00	Italy	☐ ☐	Wales	Rome
20 June, 18:00	Switzerland	☐ ☐	Turkey	Baku

Team	P	W	D	L	GD	Pts
1						
2						
3						
4						

GROUP B

12 June, 18:00	Denmark	☐ ☐	Finland	Copenhagen
12 June, 21:00	Belgium	☐ ☐	Russia	St. Petersburg
16 June, 15:00	Finland	☐ ☐	Russia	St. Petersburg
17 June, 18:00	Denmark	☐ ☐	Belgium	Copenhagen
21 June, 21:00	Finland	☐ ☐	Belgium	St. Petersburg
21 June, 21:00	Russia	☐ ☐	Denmark	Copenhagen

Team	P	W	D	L	GD	Pts
1						
2						
3						
4						

GROUP C

13 June, 18:00	Austria	☐ ☐	N Macedonia	Bucharest
13 June, 21:00	Netherlands	☐ ☐	Ukraine	Amsterdam
17 June, 15:00	Ukraine	☐ ☐	N Macedonia	Bucharest
17 June, 21:00	Netherlands	☐ ☐	Austria	Amsterdam
21 June, 18:00	N Macedonia	☐ ☐	Netherlands	Amsterdam
21 June, 18:00	Ukraine	☐ ☐	Austria	Bucharest

Team	P	W	D	L	GD	Pts
1						
2						
3						
4						

GROUP D

13 June, 15:00	England	☐ ☐	Croatia	London
14 June, 15:00	Scotland	☐ ☐	Czech Rep	Glasgow
18 June, 18:00	Croatia	☐ ☐	Czech Rep	Glasgow
18 June, 21:00	England	☐ ☐	Scotland	London
22 June, 21:00	Croatia	☐ ☐	Scotland	Glasgow
22 June, 21:00	Czech Rep	☐ ☐	England	London

Team	P	W	D	L	GD	Pts
1						
2						
3						
4						

GROUP E

14 June, 18:00	Poland	☐ ☐	Slovakia	Dublin
14 June, 21:00	Spain	☐ ☐	Sweden	Bilbao
18 June, 15:00	Sweden	☐ ☐	Slovakia	Dublin
19 June, 21:00	Spain	☐ ☐	Poland	Bilbao
23 June, 18:00	Sweden	☐ ☐	Poland	Dublin
23 June, 18:00	Slovakia	☐ ☐	Spain	Bilbao

Team	P	W	D	L	GD	Pts
1						
2						
3						
4						

GROUP F

15 June, 18:00	Hungary	☐ ☐	Portugal	Budapest
15 June, 21:00	France	☐ ☐	Germany	Munich
19 June, 15:00	Hungary	☐ ☐	France	Budapest
19 June, 18:00	Portugal	☐ ☐	Germany	Munich
23 June, 21:00	Portugal	☐ ☐	France	Budapest
23 June, 21:00	Germany	☐ ☐	Hungary	Munich

Team	P	W	D	L	GD	Pts
1						
2						
3						
4						